For Kelly and Craig and your chickens

NOTE: Children should always have adult supervision when cooking.
Do not handle any cracked or dirty eggs and wash your hands before and after
handling uncooked eggs to avoid germs that may be harmful to you.

Text and illustrations copyright © 2022 by Monica Wellington
All Rights Reserved
HOLIDAY HOUSE is registered in the U.S. Patent and Trademark Office.
Printed and bound in November 2021 at C&C Offset, Shenzhen, China.
The artwork was created with gouache.
www.holidayhouse.com
First Edition
1 3 5 7 9 10 8 6 4 2

Library of Congress Cataloging-in-Publication Data
Names: Wellington, Monica, author.
Title: Eggs from red hen farm : farm to table with mazes and maps / Monica Wellington.
Description: First edition. | New York : Holiday House, [2022] | Audience:
Ages 3–7 | Audience: Grades K–1 | Summary: "A fun story with maps and
mazes shows children where their food comes from"— Provided by publisher.
Identifiers: LCCN 2021014842 | ISBN 9780823447824 (hardcover)
Subjects: LCSH: Eggs—Juvenile literature.
Classification: LCC SF490.3 .W45 2022 | DDC 636.5/142—dc23
LC record available at https://lccn.loc.gov/2021014842

Eggs from Red Hen Farm

Farm to Table with Mazes and Maps

Monica Wellington

HOLIDAY HOUSE · NEW YORK

Let's go with Ruby and Ned

along the stone path,

past the apple trees,

the cows,

and the sunflowers,

to the henhouse.

cluck cluck

"Our chickens have certainly been busy!"

They collect eggs from every nook and cranny.

"I'm good at counting eggs," says Ned.

"I'm good at driving the red truck," says Ruby.

They are on their way,

past the ponies,

the fire station,

and the bulldozer,

to the farmers' market.

They set up their stand.
The market is open for customers.

"I'm good at counting money," says Ned.
"You take care of business here," says Ruby. "I'll make the deliveries."

She drives the red truck

across the train tracks,

onto the highway,

and over the bridge,

to the bakery in the city.

"I need those eggs!" says the baker.
"Mmm, it smells good in here!" says Ruby.

"Come by later," says the baker, "and I'll have a surprise for you!"

Ruby navigates past the post office

and the clock tower

to the school.

"Who loves fresh, tasty eggs from my farm?" Ruby asks the children.

"Let's cook together!"

Ruby drives to her next destination,

past the playground,

around the duck pond,

to the grocery store.

She delivers dozens of eggs.

The shoppers reach for them as quickly as she puts them out.
"I hope Ned is selling lots of eggs too," says Ruby to herself.

Next door, she makes her last delivery to the café.

"Perfect! I'm planning my menu," says the chef.

Ruby needs to hurry to the bakery before it closes.

"Just in time!" says the baker. "For you and Ned."

What is the quickest way
back to the farmers' market?
Ned is waiting.

"We are good at selling eggs!" they say to each other.

"Let's check on our chickens."

At last, they open their surprise!

Made with love—and eggs from Red Hen Farm! Yummy!